Welcome to your Definitive Joy in Teaching Workbook.

Your companion to the book, *Joy in Teaching*

The Definitive

Joy
IN
TEACHING
Workbook

Published by Throw Out the Box, LLC
Mount Vernon, Iowa
Design (cover and interior) and editing by Throw Out the Box, LLC
www.joyinteaching.com/workbook
ISBN:978-0-9998666-2-7

This guidebook is available at special discount when purchased in quantity. For inquiries and details contact: drcarr@joyinteaching.com

TABLE OF CONTENTS

ORIENTATION 4

REFLECTION 6

IMPACT OF TEACHER WELL-BEING 12

BURNOUT EPIDEMIC 18

BEGIN WHERE YOU STARTED 23

COMMUNITY 28

CULTURE 32

THROW OUT THE BOX 37

GET PERSONAL 42

PLANNING FOR RESILIENCE 48

LIVE WHAT YOU TEACH 55

RECLAIM THE JOY 60

SAVE THE TEACHERS 65

RESILIENCE STRATEGIES 70

PROTECTIVE PRACTICES 75

CALL TO ACTION 82

WELCOME DEDICATED EDUCATOR

The book, *Joy in Teaching*, written for you, the dedicated educator, lays out methods and provides tools that boost teacher resilience, reduce job-related stress, and support retention in the schools. This is its companion. *The Definitive Joy in Teaching Workbook* is your aide through the actionable and inspirational resources offered in Joy in Teaching.

While *Joy in Teaching* is designed to inspire reflection and motivate action, this, T*he Definitive Joy in Teaching Guidebook* is designed to walk you through the book and provide a path through discussions, exercises, and prompts to build resilience and reclaim your joy.

The book and this, its companion, is for educators who see the need for a new approach to teaching for their students and themselves. Who want to know they are not alone when teaching becomes stressful, when the profession they have dedicated their lives to begins to lose its joy. It is a beacon of light amidst the turbulent turmoil of a profession in which statistics prove has the ability to devour.

HOW TO USE THE Workbook

The Definitive Joy in Teaching Guidebook follows along with the book, *Joy in Teaching*. It lays out reflection questions, along with individual and/or group exercises and action steps for each chapter. There is space to write and reflect as you move through the book. The guidebook helps facilitate professional development by giving readers activities and talking points for discussion.

This guidebook is meant to be used, it is a tool - write in it, highlight it, scribble in the margins and let it be your guide toward a more resilient, more joyful career in education.

Whether you are working through the material by yourself, with a book study or professional learning community, or in a larger professional development scenario know that It takes reflection, planning, and work, but it's all worth it to reclaim the joy in teaching.

#SAVE the TEACHERS

- Use inventory to reflect on your current view toward your position in education.
- Analyze responses to inventory to better understand where you have the agency to create change.

Highlights from the book

- *It's important to reflect - to be clear about where you are, how you feel, and how you envision your career.*

- *It is necessary to understand where you are coming from before you plan where you are going.*

- *Just because something isn't within your complete control doesn't mean that you can't effect change. What it does mean is that you can't take on all of the responsibility and subsequent baggage by yourself.*

- *We must be careful to not diminish the spark of great teachers, but instead, foster the resiliency to maintain it.*

- *Each of the items in your inventory, the ones you have control over and the ones you don't, play a part in how you view your career in education.*

- *The following chapters will address how to build resiliency by tackling the very items you have written in your self-inventory.*

Chapter Notes & Ideas

Exercises

The self-inventory is designed to facilitate reflection and create a portrait of where you stand amidst the array of attitudes and perspectives in education. Try not to overthink. The best answers are the first ones that come into your head. Answer truthfully and thoughtfully.

Completing and reflecting on the inventory can be done in a variety of ways. Here are suggestions for guiding a group through the self-inventory exercise from Chapter 1:

- Each member completes inventory and reflection independently - this can be done before or during a group session. All members join in discussion questions and reflection of inventory experience.

- Each member completes inventory and reflection independently - this can be done before or during a group session. All members convene in small groups to share their results - followed by whole group discussion.

- Each member completes inventory and reflection separately within the group. All members convene as a whole and volunteers share inventory answers, reflection, and lessons from exercise.

- Each member completes inventory and reflection separately within the group. All members share inventory answers, reflection, and lessons as they rotate around the room.

1. Think of what you thought teaching would be like when you first set out. How has it defied your expectations?

2. What school-related thoughts keep you up at night? Or, invade your mind during your "off-duty" time?

3. What do you see as obstacles standing in the way of you best serving your students?

4. Think of what makes you feel valued as an educator. List ways you wish you would be valued.

5. What supports or resources would make you feel as if you and your students were being set up for success?

6. What are your top 3 teaching-related frustrations?

1.

2.

3.

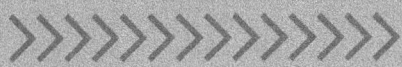

1. If you were just beginning your career in education, what advice would you give yourself?

2. What items from the self-inventory that are under your control, can you act on to improve today? What is stopping you?

3. How can recognizing which frustrations are out of your control, impact your perspective on your position as a teacher and leader?

- Define Teacher Well-being.
- Learn about research that positions teacher well-being as a priority.
- Discover how the occupational stress of a career in education spirals and impacts students and schools.

Highlights from

- *Teacher stress can equal student stress and the well-being of teachers impacts the well-being of students.*

- *Stressed teachers can negatively impact student achievement and teachers who enjoy their jobs can positively impact student achievement.*

- *If we really are behind our students and want them to succeed, we also have to be behind teachers and support their well-being by building resilience.*

- *Occupational stress and potential burnout can impact teachers' well-being in a variety of ways.*

- *Teachers are the critical, pivotal force in providing students the safe and caring learning experiences that encourage them to feel happy and successful.*

- *Good teachers should not leave the profession because they are not given the tools to manage the occupational stressors they face daily.*

Chapter Notes & Ideas

Teacher well-being

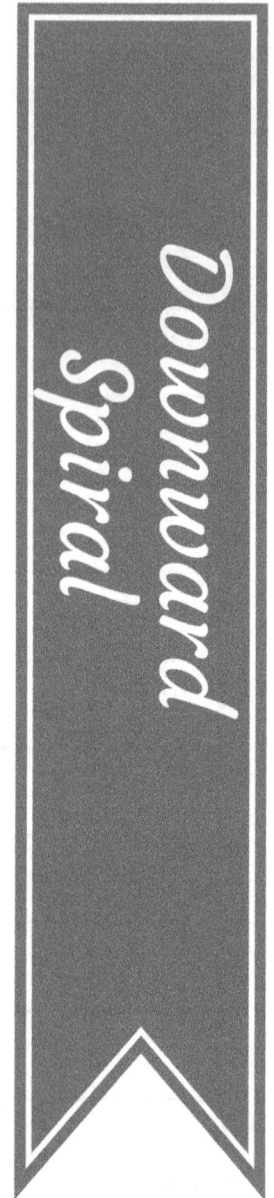

⬇

Student well-being

⬇

Student acheivement

⬇

Meeting student needs

⬇

Teacher well-being

Downward Spiral

For Your Consideration

THE DOWNWARD SPIRAL: Each level feeds the machine more. Teachers' well-being impacts students' well-being which impacts students' achievement which impacts a schools ability to meet student's needs.

Brainstorming Session

In the lines provided briefly list ideas, initiatives, and individual acts that would bolster teacher-well-being. Then rank within the squares starting with #1 for easiest to implement.

Action Plan

In groups to share your rankings and work through the Action Plan. Together develop one small way of boosting resilience in your school.

You are going to boost teacher well-being. Choose either the easiest idea (rank #1) or most interesting to you and develop an action plan.

Which idea are you choosing to implement?

What do you need to do to prepare? (think materials, people, and planning)

What are your steps for implementing this idea?

How will you know when this iniative is successful? How long do you plan this to take?

1a. How do you recognize when those around you are stressed?

1b. How can those around you know when you are stressed?

2. When you are having a bad day at work who else is impacted? How?

3. What role do you think a school should take in its teachers' well-being?

4. Consider the dynamics of where you work. What is in place to support teacher well-being?

Ch.3 Burnout Epidemic

- Review *Joy in Teaching's* Teacher Burnout Scale.
- Analyze responses to inventory to better understand where you have the agency to create change.
- Learn about the potential impact of occupational stress.
- Recognize the early warning signs of teacher burnout.

Highlights from the book

- *Teacher burnout is an insidious epidemic and we must do something about it.*

- *It takes a reexamination of school culture, a review of our own practices, and an understanding of strategies and techniques that we can use to reclaim the joy in teaching.*

- *Feeling stress does not have to mean you are headed down a path toward burnout and it certainly doesn't mean you are not an effective educator, but it does mean that your job is impacting how you feel and this should warrant some reflection.*

- *If we can give teachers the tools to recognize the early signs and symptoms of burnout then we can hope to retain good teachers by offering resources, support, and services before it's too late.*

- *Teachers care deeply and give selflessly. They deserve support in building resilience.*

Chapter Notes & Ideas

Consider the warning signs of teacher burnout, symptoms of occupational stress, and Joy in Teaching's Burnout Scale.

Group Exercise

After privately reflecting on the information in Chapter 3, share your experience. Here are some of questions to spark discusssion:

What resonates with you? Do you recognize warning signs in yourself or in those around you? What do you relate to and what do you want to avoid? What are actions you take to stay on the Passionate & Active end of the Burnout Scale. How can you (or we) reduce occupation stress.

Teacher Burnout Scale

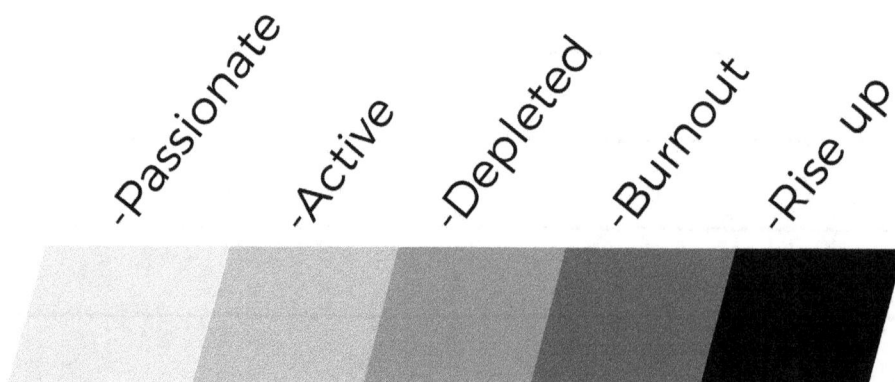

-Passionate   -Active   -Depleted   -Burnout   -Rise up

It is called a burnout scale, instead of a cycle or a timeline because it doesn't necessarily have to follow in order. You can move back-and-forth at will.

You can also use this information as a checklist to privately assess your current level of occupational stress and/or burnout.

EARLY SIGNS

of

Occupational Stress

Burnout

- **Anxiety**
  nervous, uptight, even panicky feelings, racing thoughts or a sense of worry

- **Depression**
  depletion of hope, decisiveness, confidence, motivation, even energy

- **Physical**
  muscle tightness/soreness, gastrointestinal (GI) issues, headaches, agitation, and exhaustion.

- **Behavior**
  procrastination, withdrawal, impatience and harmful habits, like over-eating, over-spending, self-medicating

- **Relationship**
  poor communication, disagreements, not listening to the needs of your partner, and anger

- *Frustration*

- *Lack of Personal*

- *Fulfillment*

- *Overwhelm*

- *Less Energy*

- *Reduced Self-Care*

- *Trouble Sleeping*

- *Negativity*

1. What are some of the avoidable causes of occupational stress and teacher burnout?

2. What are some unavoidable causes of occupational stress and teacher burnout?

3. Who can we let know, and how, when stress and or burnout begin to take hold?

4. How can we support one another when we recognize early warning signs of stress and/or burnout?

- Take time to remind yourself of the reason you got into education.
- Review the top reasons teachers enter the field.
- Recognize the power of leveraging the cycle of the school year.

Highlights from

- Taking a moment to reflect on your purpose is a simple resilience-building strategy that can make a big difference.

- How we see ourselves impacts the way we feel.

- Reconnecting with your original reasons for entering the education profession can build resilience.

- You can use the cycle of the school year and its repetitive nature to ease your stress. And, to help you thrive.

- Chances are you had some lofty idealistic goals when you started out. There is no reason that those same goals shouldn't still inspire you today. The difference is now you are making those goals happen.

- Your motivation to keep going is within you - and by looking back it becomes much, much easier to look forward.

Chapter Notes & Ideas

Take time to reconnect with the reason you entered the education profession.

Here are some of the top reasons to get you started:

Top Reasons Teachers Enter the Profession

85% To make a difference in the lives of children

74% To share a love for teaching and learning

71% To help students reach their full potential

66% To be a part of the "Aha" moments

50% Inspired by a teacher

39% To make a difference in the community

Complete the reflection on the next page and share proudly with your colleagues before engaging in the Chapter 4 Discussion Questions.

Take time to reflect on why you are here, in education, and how you got here

I was influenced to enter into a career in education by . . .

_____

_____

_____

_____

_____

_____

_____

_____

My purpose for being an educator is . . .

_____

_____

_____

_____

_____

_____

_____

_____

1. Think back to why you started. What influenced your decision to become an educator?

2. How are those influences/influencers still impacting your practices as an educator?

3. What are times of the year that you know are difficult from your own experiences that you can prepare for better?

4. What will you do to reconnect with your purpose as an educator? How will others know when you do this?

Ch.5 Community

- Discover the power of numbers through reviewing statistics on the toll of teaching.
- Consider your network of support.
- Learn the impact of a strong and supportive school community on teacher resilience.

Highlights from the book

- When teaching gets us down, we must remember we are not alone.

- Building a strong community of support within the framework of a school is one of the most powerful approaches to resilience-building.

- Building community is greatly dependent on establishing positive communication expectations and habits.

- When leaning on your community is not an option, you have to step up and take ownership of your resilience.

- Community building and support can make a significant positive difference in the climate of an entire school.

- Creating pillars of support is key.

- What a community does, that is nearly impossible to do alone, is it becomes a protective force in building resilience.

Group Exercise

Consider the climate of your school, the connections you have with your colleagues, and the community that supports you.

Reflect on how your community can and/or does boost you in light of the statistics below.

These statistics - which at surface value paint a bleak picture of the teaching profession - demonstrate an important message that we must remember as we work to build resilience and reclaim the joy in teaching. When we are stressed, overwhelmed, or even questioning our purpose - We. Are. Not. Alone.

Statistics on the Tolls of Teaching

Teachers make an average of *1500* educational decisions each day - That's 4 per minute!

The average workweek is over *50* hours

86% report having insufficient planning time

87% report that the demands of work have interfered with their personal lives

78% report feeling physically and/or emotionally exhausted at the end of the school day

45% have considered leaving the profession due to pressures related to standardized testing

37% do not plan to teach until retirement site low pay as the reason

50% leave the professional within the first *5* years
1 in *5* leave with the first *3* years

1. What are the formal professional communities you belong to (networks, cohorts, committees, etc).? How do they offer support?

2. What are the informal professional communities you belong to (those you choose to connect with about school)? How do they offer support?

3. Who can we let know, and how, when stress and or burnout begin to take hold?

4. How can we support one another when we recognize early warning signs of stress and/or burnout?

Ch.6 Culture

- Learn elements in boosting performance that the business world figured out before education.
- Discover the roles that both administrators and teachers play in developing school culture.
- Learn the key factors in establishing a positive working environment.

Highlights from

- The culture of a school exists whether we take an active role in creating it or not.

-

- Creating a culture of support can be a powerful force in retaining good teachers and helping them to reclaim their joy.

-

- Happy Employees = Better Performance.

-

- It is important for teachers and administrators to remember they are on the same team.

-

- Teachers need to see themselves as someone who can effect change to be successful.

-

- A positive school culture promotes more than just good feelings, it nurtures good behavior, creativity, problem-solving, and teacher resilience.

Chapter Notes & Ideas

school culture

Use this list to help you consider your school's culture

1. Reflect as a group on the dynamics that impact the culture.
2. Privately assess and rank the culture 1(low)-5(high).
3. Identify areas that require more attention.
4. Discuss potential changes that would benefit the culture of your school

___*Effective Leadership*

___*Supportive Environment*

___*Meaningful Connections*

___*Collaborative Colleagues*

___*Ability to Take Part in Decision-making*

___*Openness to New Ideas*

___*Regular Opportunities for Communication*

___*Willingness to Make Changes*

___*Empowered Staff*

___*Schedule*

___*Professional Development*

___*Involved Community*

Now, with the rankings and reflection from the previous page and the information below, consider the discussion questions on the next page as a group.

Key Factors in Establishing A Positive Working Environment

Setting high expectations to create a strong sense of community identity

Treating staff as professionals, with dignity and respect

Offering opportunities for teachers to affect their work through being a part of the decisionmaking

Recognizing and rewarding the efforts and achievements of staff

Scheduling regular opportunities for interaction and sharing with colleagues

Additional discussion question:
How do you see an improvment of school culture impacting you and your students each school day?

1. What do you think a stranger to your school would think of your school's culture upon first visit?

2. What do you see as your role in developing a positive school culture? Are you holding up your end?

3. What are some key areas that you feel could be addressed more in developing a positive school culture?

4. What do you see as an obstacle(s) to happiness within your position in education?
And, what can you do about it?

- Discover how a classroom that supports innovation, exploration, play, and fun can influence teacher resilience.
- Learn how developing a culture of creativity values the students and teacher as individuals.

Highlights from the book

- A culture of creativity and innovation with increased curiosity and welcomed exploration can do wonders for building resilient educators.

- Educators experience increased feelings of self-efficacy when they are willing to try new approaches and are open to offering more differentiated learning possibilities.

- A school environment that promotes resilience is one where those within feel comfortable to admit mistakes.

- When play is appropriately supported it has the potential to positively affect everyone involved.

- Teachers who actively enjoy each other's company, who can laugh together and make learning fun, are demonstrating a resilience strategy.

- If teachers and students thrive in a positive environment that values them as individuals then they will be more adept at facing challenges.

Chapter Notes & Ideas

Group Exercise

As discussed in Chapter 7, innovative, explorative, playful, and fun approaches to education can benefit both the students and the teacher.

Take time to reflect and share on how you incorporate these into your school day.

Innovation in education is an approach to teaching and learning that promotes self-efficacy and boosts interest and engagement through connecting activities to real-world experiences

How I incorporate innovation _____

_____

_____

_____

_____

_____

Exploration in education is the process of discovering the potential of an idea

How I incorporate exploration _____

_____

_____

_____

_____

_____

_____

Play in education promotes problem-solving, and critical thinking while engaging students in opportunities for social interacting and learning

How I incorporate innovation _____

_____

_____

_____

_____

_____

Exploration in education is the process of discovering the potential of an idea

How I incorporate exploration _____

_____

_____

_____

_____

_____

Group Discussions

As you share your experience and approaches to the concepts of innovation, exploration, play, and fun give feedback to one another. What ideas could be expanded or used in collaboration? What new ideas are sparked by this conversation?

1. What innovative, explorative, playful, and/or fun learning opportunities could you expand to include other disciplines? Which subjects? What would be your first steps?

2. What colleagues/department could become allies in developing collaborative and innovative learning opportunities for students?

3. What school-wide initiative could encompass all disciplines to create an opportunity for students to innovate, explore, play and have fun? What would be the first steps?

- Learn about the pressure for teachers to perform.
- Discover the impact of sharing about yourself at school.
- Use the survey to reflect on how you can bring your interests into the classroom.

Highlights from

- We don't want our teachers performing, we want them engaging.

-

- Sharing about yourself humanizes you to your students.

-

- When administrators and school leaders take time to get to really know their faculty their is a ripple effect.

-

- If, as educators, we want to prepare our students for the future and truly provide them 21st-century skills, then we have to be prepared to let go of the antiquated mindset of what learning looks like.

-

- By sharing about yourself, digging into your interests, and letting your personality shine you provide students a way to connect with you and administrators a way to acknowledge you.

-

- The ability of teachers to manage stress and navigate adverse conditions is bolstered by the knowledge that their strengths are recognized and their interests are of value.

Chapter Notes & Ideas

Interest Inventory

Fill in inventory by yourself, then join group for exercise

1. What was your favorite subject in school? What extra-curricular activities were you in?

2. What is your favorite tv and movie genres? Any stand-out favorites?

3. What do you read when you want to be entertained? Magazines, websites, apps, books...

4. What is your favorite thing to do off the "grid", no electronics or wi-fi?

5. What is your pop-culture guilty pleasure? A YA novel, a pop band, a tv show?

6. What is the thing you are best at completely outside of teaching?

Take a look at your inventory list.
Although these are your interests, this is also a list of your strengths. It showcases your personality and what you value and invest time in outside of school.

Group Exercise

Begin by sharing your inventory with those around you.
Notice how easy and fun it is to discuss these topics.
Allow sufficient time for everyone to share.

Regroup

In small groups discuss the following questions from the book:

How much of what is on this list do your students know? How much of it have you never even thought of bringing up to your students? And what would happen if you did?

How much of what is on your list does your administration know? How much of it have you never even thought of bringing up to your administration? And what would happen if you did?

Discuss in the whole group how sharing about yourself could impact the school dynamics.

1. What are some interests you could bring into school to form stronger connections with students?

2. What are some interests you could bring into school to form stronger connections with staff?

3. What are ways your interests and strengths outside of school could be put to use at school?

Ch.9 Planning for Resilience

- Learn a variety of changes you can make to your planning and practice as an educator to find more time and joy in teaching.
- Discover how knowing your strengths as a teacher can build resilience.

Highlights from the book

- Teachers need a toolbox full of strategies that set them up for success.

- You will always put students first, but placing value on your own time will help you to be the best teacher you can be.

- You are no good to your students if you are burned out - take time for yourself now.

- Providing your students more autonomy frees your time up to enjoy teaching more.

- Spreading yourself too thin or spinning your wheels in an effort to do everything only reduces your effectiveness as a teacher.

- Your goal is to ensure students learn. Let students demonstrate this through means other than testing when possible.

- By taking stock of our own strengths within the field of education we can learn to rely on the traits and abilities that will help us the most to become more resilient educators.

Group Exercise

In Chapter 9 there were a variety of ideas presented as ways to increase time and enjoy in your day-to-day routines.
Review the list below and share which ideas you see as "chance-makers" and why.

Say "No"

Protecting your time will help both you and your students.

Say "Yes"

It's not selfish to place yourself on your list of priorities.

No More Teacher Guilt

Resist the reflex to internalize it all.

Set Up Systems

Empower your students to be decision-makers & free yourself.

Practice Being Present

Multi-tasking (albeit often inevitable) is your enemy. Really.

Pick and Choose Your Extracurricular

Stay involved. But, do it with intention and value for your own time.

Formative over Summative

Let students demonstrate learning through means other than tests.

Streamline Your School Bag

If it can wait then leave it.

Batch Your Work

Group like tasks in order to cut through them quickly.

Planning Time, Tools, and Techniques

Set boundaries and priorities with your open time.

Teacher Strengths
(and potential struggles)

Consider the degree to which each of these strengths is present in your approach to teaching and learning.

The Organized Teacher

Systems, structures, and organization are where the organized teacher thrives. Their focus on preparation and planning allows them to face obstacles with a clear mind and a professional demeanor.

A plan for every situation and a place for every item is the organized teacher's dream, however, we know that teaching isn't always neat and tidy. The organized teacher can sometimes struggle a bit when things get messy and plans change quickly.

The Passionate Teacher

The passionate teacher harnesses their dedication and love for the profession to face obstacles with a sense of confidence and heart. No matter what is thrown at them, they know they can rely on their sensibilities and their instincts to get them through.

The passionate teacher is devoted to school and places their job as a top priority which is great, except sometimes carving out time for your non-work life, friends, and self can be a struggle.

The Multi-tasking Teacher

At any given time teachers have multiple plates in the air. The multi-tasking teacher smoothly juggles multiple while facing new obstacles with a sense of assurance and poise.

Although multi-tasking suites the teaching profession it is also proven to reduce productivity. Sometimes it's best to focus on one task and see it through to completion, which can be a struggle when you're accustomed to doing it all at once.

List the ways you can and/or do effect change in these categories.

Student Engagment

_____
_____
_____
_____
_____
_____
_____
_____
_____
_____

School Culture & Climate

_____
_____
_____
_____
_____
_____
_____
_____
_____
_____

Community Connections

_____
_____
_____
_____
_____
_____
_____
_____
_____

Personal Job Satisfaction

_____
_____
_____
_____
_____
_____
_____
_____
_____

1. How can we, as educators, empower ourselves to listen to our own voice? What reminders might we need?

2. When you reflect on your self-efficacy as a teacher/leader do you see yourself as someone who has the power and support to facilitate change? How so?

3. How can teacher self-efficacy be supported and heightened in your school?

4. Where (or when) in your day-to-day teaching practice do you see a need to create defined boundaries? Think time and space.

- Examine your current habits.
- Learn what is needed to make a meaningful mindset shift.
- Understand the difference in responses between a resilient and non-resilient educator.
- Discover the power of taking action toward your own joy.

Highlights from the book

- With a reexamination of habits, a strong mindset, and the resiliency tools to inspire action, teachers can reconnect with their purpose.

- Many educators are missing an essential piece of the mindset shift. Action.

- We have to provide the necessary tools and techniques to exert the extra effort that the growth mindset encourages.

- Without building strong resilience, growth mindset stays in our minds. We need action.

- By giving teachers the tools to move forward they are able to disrupt previous habits of negativity or inaction and take steps toward becoming a stronger educator.

- Resilience and teacher well-being need to be included in the everyday language of your school and deserve a seat at the professional development table.

Chapter Notes & Ideas

What are the major obstacles holding you back from thoroughly enjoying being an educator?

student behavior? scheduling? lack of recognition or autonomy? ...

Now consider how you respond to these obstacles.
Do you try to facilitate change? If so, how? if not, why not?

Evaluate your responses
What does it say about your current mindset?

Action Plan

You are going to remove an obstacle that is standing between you and the joy in teaching. You can repeat this process for each obstacle listed on the previous page.

Which obstacle do you want out of your way when it comes to enjoying your career in education?

How do you plan to change your response/ shift your mindset toward this obstacle? Do you need outside support?

How will you know when this obstacle is no longer standing in the way between you and your joy in teaching?

1. How can identifying your current habits and your compulsory responses move you forward?

2. What obstacle can you share with others to help hold yourself accountable to make a change?

3. How can colleagues support one another in a mass mindset shift toward action when it comes to building resilience and reclaiming the joy in teaching?

4. How is teacher resilience represented in professional development at your school? Where are opportunities for dialogue?

- Review the rewards and heartbreak of caring deeply.
- Understand that resilience is a learned skill.
- Discover how empowering teachers with resiliency tools reverses the negative spiral of teacher stress.
- Learn how building resilience positions you as a disruptor in the field of education.

Highlights from

-
- Teacher resilience is a learned skill - and not one often addressed in teacher education.

-
- The key is to try new ideas, take on new methods to combat the occupational stress and burnout that for far too long have been synonymous with the life of an educator.

-
- Teacher resilience positively impacts students.

-
- By reclaiming the joy in teaching and supporting those around you to do the same you are flipping the script on the current statistics of teacher burnout and the looming teacher shortage.

-
- The more a staff taps into resiliency and fosters support for teacher well-being, the more the teachers, the students, and the school as a whole benefit.

★ Feed the Spiral ★

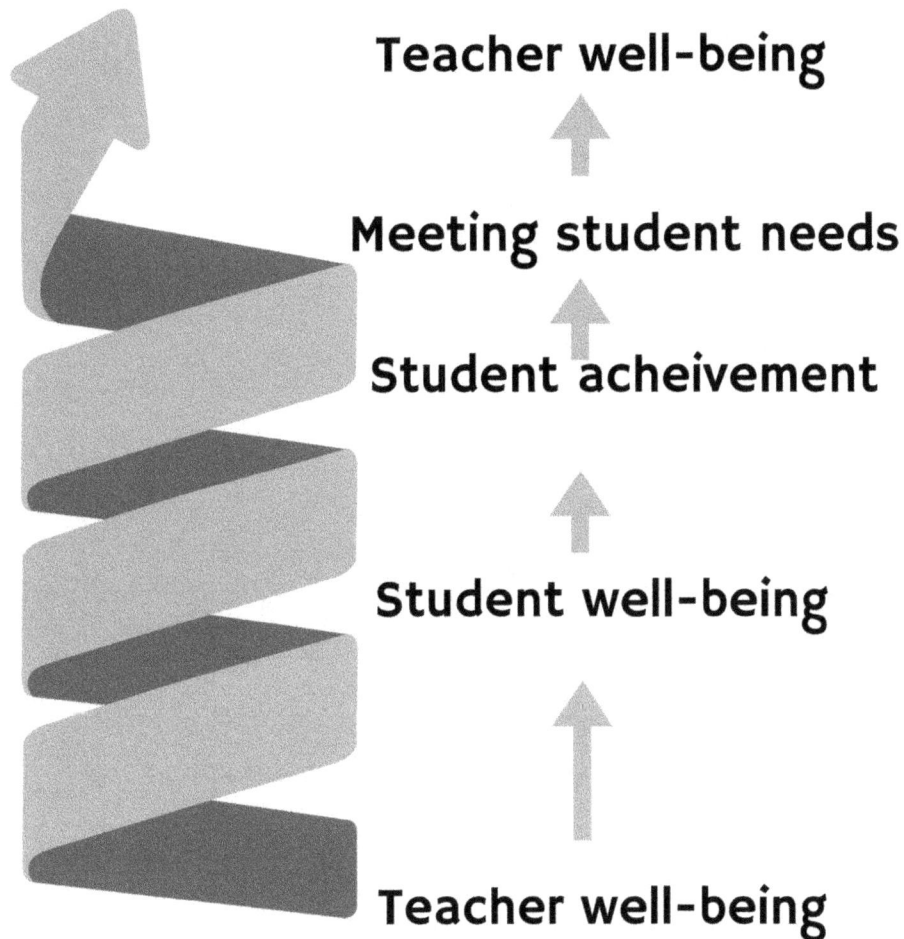

Teacher well-being

↑

Meeting student needs

↑

Student acheivement

↑

Student well-being

↑

Teacher well-being

Discussion question:

Who, what, where can you pull inspiration and strength to feed the upward spiral?

Consider your role as a disruptor -
armed with the knowledge that a resilient approach to your career in education can positively impact the success of your students and school you have the power to reverse the statistics and trends in education today.
Complete the following affirmations

As a disruptor, I can positively

influence my students lives through my _____

_____

I can motivate student success by _____

_____

I can support and uplift my colleagues by _____

_____

I can uplift my school by_____

_____

I can shift the negative trends in education by_____

_____

1. How does your resilience positively impact your students?

2. How do you envision the power of teacher resilience's ability to impact your school?

3. In what ways will you make teacher resilience a priority?

- Learn about what makes a resilience strategy.
- Review a variety of resilience strategies and how they can relieve the stress associated with a career in education.
- Consider what resilience strategies would be beneficial to your framework of action.

Highlights from the book

- Some days teaching is going to feel like work, but it's all worth it when you know your purpose, you are clear on your passion, and you are equipped with the tools to fight burnout and reclaim your joy in teaching.

- Resilience strategies as tangible, often quick, actions you can take to provide yourself a boost.

- Some of the basic building blocks of resiliency align with the necessary skills of being an educator.

- Do not discount skills that you are already familiar with as these can stand as a foundation to your framework for action.

- You can lean on the tools and techniques that you already use, whether you previously recognized resiliency skills or not.

Chapter Notes & Ideas

Develop at least one idea for how you can use each of the strategies from chapter 13 listed below. Within a group share ideas and discuss the potential of the wealth of ideas you have now that you have shared.

- **USE YOUR SENSES**

_____

_____

- **METHODS & APPROACHES**

_____

_____

- **BRING IN YOUR INTERESTS**

_____

_____

- **PROTECT YOUR TIME**

_____

_____

- **WRITE IT DOWN**

_____

_____

- **PLAN INTO THE FUTURE**

_____

_____

- **TREAT YOURSELF**

_____

_____

- **ORGANIZE YOUR SPACE**

  _____

  _____

- **BREAK YOUR ROUTINE**

  _____

  _____

- **BUDDY UP**

  _____

  _____

- **MINI-BREAKS**

  _____

  _____

- **DESIGN YOUR SPACE**

  _____

  _____

- **RANDOM ACTS OF KINDNESS**

  _____

  _____

- **GOALS**

  _____

  _____

- **CLASSROOM MINDFULNESS**

  _____

  _____

1. What resilience strategies do you already use? How can you lean on these as strengths in your framework of action?

2. What resilience strategies stand out to you as necessary in your approach to education?

3. What resilience strategies could your school adopt as a mission or group initiative to bolster staff strength?

- Learn how a protective practice differs from a resilience strategy.
- Review a variety of protective practices and how they can become a buffer between you and the occupational stress in education.
- Consider what protective practices would be beneficial to your framework of action.

Highlights from

-
- We see a need for practices that can serve as a buffer between educators and the occupational stressors they may face.

-
- Protective practices are actions you can embed into your routine.

-
- Protective practices can become habits that create long-term changes in how you relate and react to the occupational stress.

-
- It can take some to trial and error to find which protective practices work for you and your routines.

-
- Protective practices can offer more long-term solutions to occupational stress and burnout.

Chapter Notes & Ideas

Develop at least one idea for how you can use each of the practices from chapter 14 listed below. Within a group share ideas and discuss the potential of the wealth of ideas you have now that you have shared.

- **DEEP BREATHING**

- **SELF-TALK**

- **PROGRESSIVE MUSCLE RELAXATION**

- **REFLECTION**

- **YOGA**

- **MEDITATION**

- **VISUALIZATIONS**

- **AVOIDANCE OF STRESS DRIVERS**

- **RELY ON YOUR STRENGTHS**

  _____

  _____

- **HEALTHFUL LIFESTYLE**

  _____

  _____

- **PURPOSE**

  _____

  _____

- **SUPPORT SYSTEM**

  _____

  _____

- **CLEAR BOUNDARIES**

  _____

  _____

- **CONTENT KNOWLEDGE**

  _____

  _____

- **POSITIVE OUTLOOK**

  _____

  _____

- **TEACHER MINDSET**

  _____

  _____

- **PRIORITIZE**

  _____

  _____

- **PROFESSIONAL ASSISTANCE**

  _____

1. What protective practices stand out to you as necessary in your approach to education?

2. Consider the protective practices you have chosen to implement. How can you transform these practices into habits of your daily life?

3. Are there any protective practices that could become part of a school improvement plan/school-wide initiative? How?

Call to Action

- Determine what strategies fit best for you.
- Consider how you know when you are stressed.
- Develop a plan for when you will use your resiliency strategies.
- Remember your purpose.
- Seek the joy in teaching.

Highlights from the book

Develop tiers of resilience strategies, ones for when things are going well and others for when stress beings to take hold.

You are the best judge of how things are going. Listen to yourself, to your body and your mind.

Stress is normal, it can even be healthy.

By listening to yourself you can make the necessary adjustments to your routine quickly and avoid moving down The Teacher Burnout Scale.

Ask yourself the tough questions now so that when those hectic school days come, as we know they will, you do not have to think about how you will react.

Rely on your resilience-building skills and keep your eyes open for the joy, because it is there, every day.

MY ACTION PLAN

My purpose as an educator

How I will take care of myself when being a teacher is going well

List your resilience strategies and protective practices

How will I know when I am stressed and need to use new resiliency skills

List your warning signs to stress

How I will take care of myself when being a teacher is stressful

List your resilience strategies and protective practices

What I will remind myself when things become overhwhelming

Write what motivates you

81

Looking for more?

WWW.JOYINTEACHING.COM

WWW.TIFFANYCARR.COM

DRCARR@JOYINTEACHING.COM

If you have enjoyed this book please recommend it to your colleagues & leave a positive review on www.amazon.com

◇ THROW OUT THE BOX

CREATE. INNOVATE. COLLABORATE. SUCCEED.

A publisher for schools, businesses, and professionals

www.throwoutthebox.com